AN

AUTHENTIC ACCOUNT

OF THE

REDUCTION

OF

LOUISBOURG,

In *June* and *July* 1758.

Ob Patriam pugnando. —— VIRG.

By a SPECTATOR.

The Naval & Military Press Ltd

Published by
The Naval & Military Press Ltd

In reprinting in facsimile from the original, any imperfections are inevitably reproduced and the quality may fall short of modern type and cartographic standards.

THE

READER

MAY depend on the *Impartiality* of theſe *Minutes*, as the Writer, though preſent the whole Time, neither was himſelf an *Actor* in any Thing he relates, nor under any *Influence* from Dependance or Connexion with thoſe that were. And, the *Authenticity* of the Whole may be as far relied on, as it is poſſible to credit the concurrent Accounts of ſeveral *Gentlemen*, who were preſent at its different Parts, and related them regularly as they were tranſacted.

Theſe

Theſe Accounts were at firſt collected, only for the Satisfaction of ſome *Friends*; and are now communicated for the Information of the *Public*, becauſe they have none that are better. It is hoped, they will contribute to give the Reader a juſt Opinion of all thoſe *brave* Men, who *directed* and *aſſiſted* in the *Reduction of Louiſbourg*.———

Quique ſui Memores *alios fecere* merendo.

MINUTES

Concerning the REDUCTION of

LOUISBOURG.

THE Commanding Officers in the *Expedition* against this important *Fortreſs*, were theſe that follow;

Of the *Fleet*.

The Honble *Edward Boſcawen*, Admiral of his Majeſty's *Blue* Squadron, and Commander in Chief of all his Majeſty's Ships and Veſſels employed, and to be employed, in *North America*.

Sir *Charles Hardy*, Knt. Rear Admiral of the *White*.

Philip Durell, Eſq; Commodore.

Of the *Army*.

Major-General *Jeffery Amherſt*, Commander in Chief of his Majeſty's Forces to be employed in the Iſland of *Cape Breton*, &c.

Brigadier-General *Edward Whitmore*.

Brigadier-General *Charles Laurence*.

Brigadier-General *James Wolfe*.

Colonel *Baſtide*, Chief Engineer.

The *Fleet* conſiſted of the following Ships.

Ships	Guns.	Commanders
Namur	90	Honble *Edw. Boſcawen*, eſq; Captain *Buckle.*
Royal William	84	Sir *Charles Hardy*, Knt. Captain *Evans.*
Princeſs Amelia	80	*Philip Durell*, Eſq; Captain *Bray.*
Dublin	74	Capt. *Rodney*
Terrible	74	*Collins.*
Northumberland	70	R^{t} Honble Ld *Colvil.*
Vanguard	70	*Swanton.*
Orford	70	*Spry.*
Burford	70	*Gambier.*
Somerſet	70	*Hughes.*
Lancaſter	70	Honble *Geo. Edgecumbe*
Devonſhire	66	*Gordon.*
Bedford	64	*Fowke.*
Captain	64	*Amherſt.*
Prince Frederick	64	*Man.*
Pembroke	60	*Simcoe.*
Kingſton	60	*Parry.*
York	60	*Pigot.*
Prince of Orange	60	*Ferguſon.*
Defiance	60	*Baird.*
Nottingham	60	*Marſhall.*
Centurion	54	*Mantell.*
Sutherland	50	*Rous.*

Frigates.

Juno, Diana, Boreas, Trent, Gramont, Shannon, Hind, Portmahon, Nightingale, Kennington, Squirrel, Beaver, Hunter, Scarborough, Hawke, Ætna, Lightening, Tyloe.

The

The Army confifted of the following Regiments.

Commanding Officers Names.	Regimts	Battals.	Colonel	Lt.Cols	Majors	Capts	Lieuts.	Enfigns	Chapls	Adjuts	Q. Maft	Surgns	SurgM.	Serjnts	Drum.	Rank and File.
Lieutenant-General *James St. Clair*,	1	2		1	1	7	20	9	1	1	1	1	2	38	18	854
Major-General *Jeffery Amherft* —— ——	15			1	1	8	18	7	1	1	1	1	2	35	19	763
Brigadier General *John Forbes* ——	17			1	1	7	10	9		1	1	1	1	29	20	660
Brigadier-General *Edward Whitmore*, —— ——	22			1		8	17	8		1	1	1	2	37	20	910
Lieutenant-General *Philip Brag* —— ——	28			1	1	7	9	8	1	1	1	1	1	30	20	627
Lieutenant-General *Charles Otway*, —— ——	35			1		5	12	5		1	1	1	1	20	14	566
Major-General *Peregrine Thomas Hopfon*, ——	40			1		7	16	6		1	1	1	2	30	16	655
Lieutenant-General *Hugh Warburton*, ——	45			1	1	7	17	6		1	1	1	1	38	19	852
Lieutenant-General *Peregrine Lafcelles*, ——	47			1	1	5	15	9		1	1	1	2	38	18	856
Colonel *Daniel Webb*, —— —— ——	48			1	1	7	16	8	1	1	1	1	2	38	20	932
Colonel *Robert Anftruther* —— —— ——	58			1		8	8	7		1	1	1	1	26	15	615
Honourable Colonel *Robert Monckton* ——	60	2			1	6	20	7		1	1	1	2	39	20	925
Brigadier-General *Charles Laurence*, —— ——	60	3	1		1	6	16	7			1	1	2	35	17	814
Colonel *Simon Frazier* of the *Highlanders*, ——	63			1	1	10	22	10	1	1	1	1	2	43	22	1084
Lieutenant-Col. *George Scott* of the Five Companies of *Rangers*,				1		5	12	5				1		24	2	499
Effective Total	1		1	13	10	103	228	111	5	13	14	15	23	507	260	11,602

The Train of Artillery commanded by Colonel *George Williamfon*.

	Colonel.	Captains.	Capt. Lts.	1ft Lieuts.	2d Lieuts.	Lt. Firew,	Adjutant	Qu. Maftr	Surgeons.	Serjeants.	Corporals	Bombard	Gunners	Matroffes.	Miners.	Drummer	Effective Total.
Chief Engineer Colonel *Baftide*.	1	3	2	6	5	4	1	1	2	11	14	28	63	165	11	7	324

On the 28th of *May*, 1758, Admiral *Boscawen* sailed from *Halifax* Harbour with the *Squadron* he brought from *England*, and the Transports with the *Forces* under his Convoy; and on,

June 2. Anchored them in *Gabreuse* Bay, in the Island of *Cape Breton*, above three Leagues by Sea from the Harbour of *Louisbourg* to the South West of it.

In the Evening the *General*, with the Brigadier-Generals *Laurence* and *Wolfe*, reconnoitred the Shore as near as possible, and made a Disposition for landing in *three* Places. They observed that the Enemy had a *Chain* of *Posts* along the Shore from *Cape Noir* to *Flat-Point*, and Irregulars from thence to the Bottom of the Bay; with Works and Batteries at all the Places where it was probable or practicable for any Troops to land.

3. They discovered several *Encampments* of the Enemy along the Shore of a little Bay, at the N. E. End of *Gabreuse*, which was the most convenient Place for the intended Descent: This Bay has since been called *Kennington Cove*, from that *Frigate*'s being stationed there as closely as she could venture to the Shore to play her Cannon upon the Enemy and their Batteries on the Day of landing the Troops.

Brigadier General *Whitmore* arrived this Day from *Halifax*. As less *Surf* was observed in one Cove than the others, a Disposition was this Day made to land at that *one* Place, instead of the *three* proposed yesterday.

4. We had a thick Fog, and so hard a Gale, that the *Trent* Frigate struck on a Rock, made repeated Signals of Distress, and unshiped her Rudder; but, with much Difficulty, was got off. The *Transports* were in great danger of driving on Shore,

Shore, having ſuffered a good deal in their Cables and Anchors, in the rocky part of the Bay, in which they rode at that time for the Conveniency of their Situation to the Shore, where the landing was propoſed.

June 5. Was a Day of thick Fog, with ſo great a *Surf* driving on the Shore, that nothing could be attempted.

6. After ſome Rain and Fog in the Morning, it was judged proper on an Appearance of Change of Weather to make an Attempt of landing the Troops. Accordingly after the Signal made, the Boats they were debarked into, rowed towards the Shore: But, on the Report of ſome Captains of the Fleet, who were ordered to reconnoitre the Beach, that the *Surf* was then too high, the Troops reimbarked in their reſpective Tranſports.

7. When the Fog cleared up, we ſound that the Surf was too high for the Troops to make any Attempt of landing this day.

But, in hopes of better Weather the next Morning, a Regiment was ſent, by the Mouth of the Harbour, in a Number of Sloops, with a Proportion of Artillery, to make a Shew of landing at *Lorembec*; but not actually to land there till farther Orders, the *General* intending only to draw the Enemy's Attention that way, to facilitate his intended Landing at the N. E. end of *Gabreuſe* Bay.

Almoſt every Day ſince they had been at Anchor, ſome of the *Frigates* fired at Parties of the Enemy they ſaw near the Shore, it was thought, with ſome Effect.

8. About 2 o'Clock in the Morning the Troops were debarked into the *Men of War* and the *Tranſports* Boats, rowed by their proper Crews; the *former* under the Direction of a *Lieutenant*, *Mate*, or

June 8. or *Midſhipman*, and the *latter* under that of the *Officer* of the Troops in each Boat. The following is the *Order* of *landing*, in three *Diviſions*, given by the General, for preſerving the greater Regularity:

Amherſt's.	Otway's	Hopſon's	Laurence's	Warburton's	Whitmore	Left Brigades Right	Forbes's	Webb's	Monckton's	Anſtruther	Laſcelles's	Royals.

Light Infantry and Frazier's	To draw up to the left of Amherſt's.	To draw up to the right of the Royals	Brag's Regiment.

With Directions to obſerve, if poſſible, the following *Method* of marching the Troops *after* their *Landing*;

Amherſt's	Whitmore's	Otway's	Warburton's	Webb's	Monckton's	Frazier's	Grenadiers.	Laurence's	Anſtruther's	Laſcelles's	Hopſon's	Brag's	Forbes's	Royals.

Light Infantry & Fraſr's	Regiments of the Left Brigade,				Regiments of the Right Brigade,				Brag's Regiment,
	Amhſt's	Hopſon's	Laur.	Otw's	Laſc.	Monckt	Anſtr	Royals	

Regiments of the ſecond Line		Regiments of the ſecond Line,	
Whitmore's	Warburton's	Webb's	Forbes's

Previous to the landing, Capt. *Rous* in the *Sutherland* and ſeveral other *Frigates*, had, by the Admiral's Direction, ſtationed themſelves as near the Shore as was convenient, to terrify and annoy the Enemy's fortified Encampments, the better to prepare for the Attempt of the Boats.

Their Diſpoſition was—the *Sutherland* and *Squirrel* on the Right near *White Point*; the *Kennigton* and *Halifax Snow* on the Left near *Kennington Cove*; and the *Grammont*, *Diana* and *Shannon* Frigates in the

the *Centre*. Accordingly, after Commodore *Durell* *June* 8. had reported it as his Opinion, that the Troops might land on the *Left*, without any great Interruption from this Morning's Surf, about *Sun-riſe* this Day a moſt furious cannonading was begun by the *Kennington* and *Halifax Snow*, which was continued by all the reſt with only ſome neceſſary Intermiſſions in Favour of the Attempt, until about 8 o'Clock. About 4 this Morning under Cover of the Ship's Guns, the Boats with a *Diviſion* of the Troops, after a general Rendezvous near *White Point*, made an *Attempt* of landing to the Left at *Kennington Cove*, with 600 *Light Infantry*, the whole Battalion of *Highlanders*, and 4 Companies of *Grenadiers*, under the Command of Brigadier General *Wolfe*; while a *Feint* of landing was made to the Right towards *White Point*, conducted by Brigadier General *Whitmore*; and the Brigades in the Centre were commanded by Brigadier General *Laurence*, who made a Shew of landing at the *Freſh-Water Cove*, the more to diſtract the Enemy's Attention, and to divide their Force.

The *left* Wing, finding the Shore at *Kennington Cove* impregnable, withdrew with ſome Loſs from the warm Fire of two *Batteries* diſcharging Grape and round Shot upon them in flank; while ſeveral *Swivels*, and ſmall Arms almoſt without Number ſhowered on them from the *Lines*, that were about 15 feet above the Level of the Boats. As the Enemy had for ſome *Years* been preparing againſt ſuch a probable Attempt; they had now been ſome *Days* in Expectation of our Viſit: They had accordingly poſted themſelves along the Shore to the Number of more than 3000 Regulars, Irregulars, and a few of the native *Indians*, in all the probable Places of landing, behind a very ſtrong *Breaſt-*

June 8. *Breast-work*, fortified at proper Distances with several Pieces of *Cannon*, besides *Swivels* of an extraordinary Calibre, mounted on very strong perpendicular Stocks of Wood, driven deep into the Ground: They had also prepared for flanking, by erecting *Redans* mounted with Cannon in the most advantageous Situations—Nothing of the Kind has perhaps been seen more complete than these *Fortifications*. Besides, all the Approaches to the *Front-Lines* were rendered so extremely difficult by the *Trees* they had laid very thick together upon the Shore round all the *Cove*, with their Branches lying towards the Sea, for the Distance of 20 in some, and of 30 Yards in other places, between the Lines and the Water's Edge; that, had our People not been exposed to such a *Fire* from the Enemy, the bare Attempt of possessing these Lines, would have been like that of travelling towards them thro' a *wild Forest*, from the interwoven Branches of one Tree to those of another with incredible Fatigue and endless Labour.

Nor, was this Stratagem possible to be suspected at any great Distance, as the Place had the Appearance of one continued *Green* of little scattered Branches of Fir. And, but very few of the Guns on their Lines were to be distinguished out of the Reach of their Metal; the rest were artfully concealed from our View with *Spruce-Branches*, until the Boats advanced towards the Shore with the Resolution of *forcing* the Works—The latent Destruction was then *unmasked*, by the Removal of the *Spruce-Branches*, and the adventurous Spectators were soon convinced, those Works were not *capable* of being *forced* by Numbers much superior to theirs. The Enemy *depended* much on their Strength here, which perhaps occasioned them to be somewhat

what *premature* in their Exertion of it: For, before our Boats came near the Water's Edge, they began with great Alertneſs to play their Batteries, and to fire *red hot* Balls, beſides a continual Diſcharge of their ſmall Arms among them. The Conſequence had been much more fatal to our People, few if any of whom would have eſcaped, had the Enemy timed their Fire with more Judgment, by permitting the Boats to have actually landed their Men on that narrow ſhoal Beach, taking no other Notice of them until they had been all in their Power, than they had done before of the Fire from our *Frigates*, and of ſome *Boats* that had been with Commodore *Durell* to reconnoitre the Shore, before any of the Troops had put off from the Tranſports. *June* 8.

Exaſperated, not diſcouraged, at this Repulſe from the Enemy's irreſiſtible Fire, the Troops of that *Wing* drew off with all convenient Expedition towards the *Centre*, determined to ruſh on Shore wherever they ſaw any Probability of Succeſs, whatever Loſs they might ſuſtain. Soon after this, the Lieutenants *Browne* and *Hopkins*, with Enſign *Grant* and about 100 of the *Light Infantry* happily gained the Shore over almoſt impracticable Rocks and Steeps to the Right of the *Cove*. Upon which, Brigadier *Wolfe* directed the Remainder of this Command to puſh on Shore as ſoon as poſſible, and as well as they could—which heightened their eager Impatience ſo much, that the *Light Infantry*, *Highlanders* and *Grenadiers* intermixed, ruſhed forward with impetuous Emulation, without Regard to any previous Orders, and piqued themſelves mightily which Boat could be moſt dexterous and active in getting firſt on Shore. In this manner,

June 8. though all the while exposed to the Fire of a Battery of *three Guns*, that sometimes raked, sometimes flanked their Boats very furiously, and of small Arms within 20 Yards of them, they were all expeditiously landed with little Loss, besides about 22 Grenadiers, who were unfortunately drowned, by having their Boats stove in the bold Attempt.

Among the foremost of these Parties was Brigadier *Wolfe*, who jumped out of his Boat into the Surf to get to the Shore, and was readily followed by Numbers of the Troops, amidst a most obstinate Fire of the Enemy. Soon after landed Brigadier *Laurence*, and was followed by the rest of the Brigades with all possible Expedition. After him in a little time Brigadier *Whitmore*, and the Division of the right Wing, gained the Shore amidst a continual Charge of Shot and Shells from the Enemy's *Lines*, several of the latter reaching also as far as the Brigades in the Centre. And, last of all landed the Commander in Chief Major-General *Amherst* in the Rear, full of the highest Satisfaction from seeing the Resolution, Bravery and Success of the Troops in surmounting *Difficulties* and despising *Dangers*. A noble Specimen of the *Spirit* he had to depend on their exerting, in the Course of this Undertaking; where they must expect to encounter so many of the *one* and of the *other*. In short, never perhaps might this Observation be more justly applied to the heroic Bravery and Conduct of *English Officers* and *Soldiers*, than on this remarkable Occasion—*Regis ad Exemplum totus componitur Orbis.*

It would be an injurious Diminution of the *Glory* our landing Parties acquired in this hazardous Enterprize, not to remark particularly the *Difficulties* they had to surmount.—Such a boisterous *Surf* drove

drove on most Parts of the Shore at that time as *June* 8. stove a great Number of their Boats, by which several of the Men were so much hurt and bruised, as to be very incapable of helping and taking Care of themselves, and some Others were crushed to pieces between the Boats and the Rocks. Most, if not all of those who did land, were obliged to wade through the great Swell, themselves and their *Arms* much wetted; and after that, to scramble up such rugged *Rocks*, and almost perpendicular *Precipices* as to the wary Enemy's *Engineers* seemed in need of no *Fortification* or *Defence*, their own steep, rough Ascent having been judged beyond the Attempt of Men under Arms before this *glorious* Morning. And, to complete the discouraging Scene, they were all the while exposed to the utmost Fury of the Enemy's *Fire*, and not in a Situation of exerting themselves in any Kind of *Defence*, except by *terrifying* the astonished Foe with the resolute Bravery of gaining what had till now been thought an inaccessible Shore, and landing in the most unexpected, one who had not the strongest Proofs of the Fact might say, incredible Places. But none, nor even all these Discouragements were able to damp the truly *English Spirit* of our People in this brave Attempt—A *national Spirit* that our Soldiery are never known to want under the Conduct of such Commanders as signalized themselves here—a *Spirit* that will give both the *Officers* and *Soldiers* of this *memorable Day* an honourable Distinction among *Englishmen*, as long as *British Bravery* shall be successful in the Defence of *British Liberty*.

The Spirit and Fortitude, which thus visibly actuated all these Troops in this heroic Attempt, no less remarkably distinguished their whole suceeeding Conduct; which was but one continued Exer-

June 8. tion of the greatest Bravery. They instantly attacked the next *Battery* to them in flank with so much Vigour, as soon forced a numerous Body of the Enemy to abandon their strong Post with great Precipitation. And, so great was the Resolution they shewed in surrounding and attacking the Enemy's extensive *Lines*, that they had hardly given there a Specimen of true *English* Bravery, before they saw themselves left *Masters* of the Shore with all its strong Works. The dastardly *Panic* that appeared to slacken the Enemy's Fire as soon as they saw our Men landed pretty near them, now shewed itself very conspicuously by its Effects, the little Resistance they made when their Numbers are compared with ours, and the great Confusion with which they fled every way before our Men into the contiguous Woods; while several of them were killed in their Flight, and upwards of 70 taken Prisoners: Among these were two *Captains* of Grenadiers and two *Lieutenants*, who with the Men were immediately sent on board the Fleet. The *French* Officer that commanded here was, Lieutenant Col. *M. St. Julien.* Our *General Officers* were all this time remarkably active: And, it would be an Injustice to their *Merits* not to say, that we owe this Success chiefly to their animating Presence and prudent Conduct.

The Enemy's Flight was the more precipitate, from an Apprehension, that Brigadier *Whitmore*, who had landed the Troops on the Right, would attempt to cut off their Retreat into the Garrison of *Louisbourg*; which must then have soon fallen into our Hands, as there were not, by their own Accounts since, above 300 Men left in it that Morning, the rest having been drawn to the Shore to oppose our landing: For, they well knew, that the

the Succefs of their Efforts there, was effectually to decide the Fate of *Louisbourg*; which is not tenable for any long time againft a numerous *Army* with a good Train of *Artillery*, affifted and fupported by fuch a *Fleet* as we had fo near at hand. *June* 8.

After this fignal *Succefs*, which exceeded our moft fanguine Expectations, the Troops were difpofed in fuch a manner, as at once to poffefs the *Shore*, and to purfue the *Enemy*. The Party that remained at the Water-fide, fecured the Poffeffion of the Shore all the Way to *Louifbourgh* for feveral Miles in Length, and found in different Places abandoned by the flying Enemy, feveral Arms, a good Quantity of Provifions and Ammunition, 17 Pieces of Cannon, and 14 large Swivels; a Furnace for red hot Balls, and two Mortars, one of Brafs of 8 Inches, and another of Iron of 10 Inches Diameter, with a Shell in it ready to be fired—but its late Mafters were in too much Hurry. Among the *Slain* was one *Officer*, and a native *Indian* Chief, a very ftout, well made, and, as fome of our Troops can witnefs, a very active, intrepid Man, with a *Medal* of Diftinction from the *French King*, hung round his Neck, which was prefented to Admiral *Bofcawen*.

The other Party that was imployed in the Purfuit of the difperfed Enemy, under the Command of the Brigadiers *Laurence* and *Wolfe*, drove them over rocky Hills and boggy Moraffes for Security under the Cannon of *Louisbourg*, by 10 o'Clock the fame Morning. The Purfuit concluded with the Difcharge of feveral Pieces of Cannon from the *Ramparts* of the Town towards our Troops; which did them no *Damage* at all, and were of fingular *Service*, in pointing out to the *General Officers* the *Diftance* from the Town, where they could encamp with

June 8. with Security to invest it. Soon after, the *Garrison* took the seasonable Precaution of setting Fire to the Barracks at the *Grand Battery*, which they had before dismantled and ruined; and of destroying all their Out-buildings in one general Conflagration, which made a prodigious Blaze all that Afternoon, and a great Part of the Night; and left nothing standing within two Miles of the Town-Walls, but the Towers at the *Grand Battery*, and some Chimneys and Gable Ends of their wretched Hovels. The Persuers that very Afternoon, after reconnoitring the Ground, marked out the Camp, which our Army afterwards occupied during the whole Siege.

The *Prisoners* we made at landing said, that the greatest Part of our Business was done, in the landing of our Troops; which their *Engineers* had before assured the *Governor* of *Louisbourg*, was impossible for almost any Number of Men to do—and that none, but Madmen, would have attempted it, where the *English* did. Our *Light Infantry*, *Highlanders* and *Rangers* they termed *the English Savages*, perhaps in Contradistinction to their own native *Indians*, *Canadians*, &c. *the true French Savages.* These *Light Infantry* were a Corps of 550 Volunteers chosen as Marksmen out of the most active resolute Men from all the Battalions of *Regulars*, dressed some in *blue*, some in *green Jackets* and *Drawers*, for the easier brushing through the Woods; with *Ruffs* of black Bear's Skin round their Necks, the Beard of their upper Lips, some grown into *Whiskers*, others not so, but all well *smutted* on that part; with little *round Hats* like several of our Seamen—Their *Arms* were a Fusil, Cartouch-Box of Balls and Flints, and a Powder horn flung over their Shoulders. The *Rangers* are a Body of

Irregulars, who have a more cut-throat, *ſavage* *June* 8. Appearance; which carries in it ſomething of *natural* Savages: The Appearance of the *Light Infantry* has in it more of *artificial* Savages.

The Day of landing Sir *Charles Hardy*, with his Squadron, joined Mr. *Boſcawen*'s in *Gabreuſe Bay*, from his ſevere Cruize on this Coaſt ever ſince the Beginning of *April*. Some of his Ships had ſuffered ſo much in their Men, chiefly by the Scurvy, that they wanted Aſſiſtance to bring them to an Anchor in the Bay—the greater Part of them recovered apace when put on Shore.

In the Harbour of *Louiſbourg* we ſaw five or ſix large Ships of the *Line*, beſides about as many *Frigates* that had eſcaped the conſtant Vigilance of Sir *Charles*'s Squadron, ſome in Snow-Storms, others in thick foggy Weather, ſo well known to all that have cruized upon the Coaſt at that Seaſon of the Year.

As your Ignorance of it may betray you, like many others of our Friends in the Country into the Abſurdity of ſuppoſing Sir *Charles*'s Cruize there with his Squadron little more than as an Officer with a Party of Soldiers poſted on the Side of a *Turn-pike Road*, in ſight of the *Gate*, to watch a Party of the Enemy expected to paſs that way; whom if he does not ſurprize, you will ſay he has not done his Duty like a good Officer. Let me tell you, not only that the Coaſt is *extenſive*, and that *Winds* and *Currents* would not always permit him to keep his Station—but even, when he could keep it, the *Snow-Storms* and *Fogs* often prevented our ſeeing any Objects at the Diſtance of our Ship's Length. You will be eaſier convinced of this, by an Inſtance of each.——

The

June 8. The 27th of *April* was a Day of ſuch *Rime* and Storms of *Snow*, that we could not ſee one of our own Squadron but once, towards the Evening. The Method of keeping Ships together on ſuch Occaſions, is either by *lying-to*, or by firing *Fog-Guns* every half hour that they make Sail. *Le Prudent* and ſome other *French* Men of War, having made the Land the Day before, ſtole unperceived along Shore to the Mouth of *Louiſbourg* Harbour, with the greateſt Security, from having heard our *Fog-Guns* at a Diſtance, as they have ſince told us. Now, what *Prudence* or *Vigilance* could poſſibly have prevented what, you ſee, was out of the Power of both?

Let me add another Inſtance to give you ſome Idea of the Thickneſs of the *Bank-Fogs* on the Coaſt of *Cape-Breton*—In the Night of the 5th of *May* we had ſo ſevere a Froſt, that the next Morning all our Rigging was caſed over with ſuch a thick *Ice*, that it was not capable of being worked, till the Ice was beaten off from the Ropes, which took up ſeveral hours of that Forenoon. That *Ice* was nothing elſe but *congealed Fog*, as we had no Rain or Snow the whole Night. Our Officers computed the Quantity of Ice beaten off from the Rigging of our ſingle Ship, between 6 and 8 Tun Weight. After this, you will not be ſurprized at my telling you, that we were for 16 Days together without Sight of Land, on Account of the Thickneſs of the Fog, though we were every Day within a proper Diſtance to ſee it, had the Air been tolerably clear. On ſuch a Coaſt, what can the niceſt Vigilance do, without ſuch a Number of Ships as might form a Line of almoſt equal Length to it?

9. The Remainder of the Troops were debarked from the Tranſports, that could not conveniently be

be landed the Day before, and were not judged immediately neceſſary to be ſent for, from the extraordinary Succeſs of the Parties who firſt landed. The Sloops ſent the 7th returned from *Lorembec*, with the Troops and Artillery.—There was a *Lieutenant Colonel's* Command poſted in and round *Kennington Cove*, to guard the Shore againſt the accidental Incurſions of the *Savages* from the adjacent Woods: Others of the Troops were ſtationed at proper Diſtances on ſomewhat of a Road through the Woods, to keep the Communication open and uninterrupted between the Shore and the Ground that had the Day before been marked out for the Camp: The reſt were imployed in clearing the Camp Ground. There were, beſides ſeveral Out-Centinels, Parties of *Light Infantry* and *Rangers* ordered to patrole round the Rear of the Camp from the left Wing to the Back of the Poſt at *Kennington Cove*, to prevent all Surprize and Diſturbance from lurking *Indians*, *Canadians* that were expected, or any ſcattered Parties of the Enemy that might have been cut off from the Garriſon the Day before, or occaſionally detached out of it afterwards. *June* 9.

The great Surf this Day interrupted the landing the Baggage, &c. This Day ſome Troops from *France* to the Number of 400 Men, part of the Regiment of *Cambiſe* got into the Garriſon, as we afterwards learned: They were landed at the Harbour of St. *Anne* in the N. E. part of the Iſland of *Cape Breton* out of 4 or 5 Men of War, who ſoon made the beſt of their way off, but whither, we could not be informed. Theſe, we were told, were the ſame Ships that had been chaſed towards the Shore laſt Spring in the *Bay* of *Biſcay* by Sir *Edward Hawke's* Squadron.

June. 10. Our Troops were imployed in clearing the Camp Ground, pitching of Tents and carrying the Baggage, &c. that had been landed by the remaining Boats of the Men of War and Tranſports. This Day the Surf was a great Interruption to the landing of Stores. There was, every Day that would permit, one of the Captains of the *Line of Battle* Ships ordered to inſpect and direct the landing of all the *Stores* and *Artillery* from the Tranſports neceſſary for the Camp, and to attend this Duty until it was over, in a continued Rotation, according to their *Seniority*. The turbulent Surf almoſt continually driving on the Shore, made this a very troubleſome Employment to the *Directors*, and very haraſſing to the *Seamen*; ſwamped and ſtove many of the *Boats*, and was ſome Days ſo great as to put it out of the Power of any Boats to get on Shore.

This Afternoon Sir *Charles Hardy*, by Signal from the Admiral, ſlipped his Cable, ſailed from *Gabreuſe Bay* with 7 or 8 Ships of the Line under his Command, and anchored off the Mouth of *Louiſbourg* Harbour; to prevent, if poſſible, the *French* Squadron from getting out to Sea, whenever they might be diſpoſed to improve the Opportunity of a fair Wind in a dark Night or a Fog, to ſave their Ships from falling into our Hands.

11. Our Troops were employed as the Day before, and began to make *Roads* in the Camp over *Rocks* and *Moraſſes*, otherwiſe impaſſable by Carriages, and hardly paſſable by the Men without any Burden at all. This Day a *Serjeant Major* of *Fiſcher*'s Regiment of *Volontairs Etrangers*, with 4 of the Men, deſerted from the *Garriſon*, and gave us Intelligence, that their Number did not exceed 4000, and including the *Inhabitants* that bore Arms, not 5000 Men—that the greateſt part of

of this Regiment were ſo well diſpoſed to deſert, that they only watched an Opportunity to quit a Place and Service they had been trepanned into, contrary to the Promiſes made to them at their inliſting in the *French* Service—and that the Enemy had deſtroyed the *Grand* and *Light-houſe* Batteries, and called in all their Out-Poſts. Some light 6 pounders that were expected to follow the landing of the *Troops*, could not be got on Shore till now; when ſome *Artillery Stores* were brought along with them.

12. About 2 o'Clock in the Morning Major *Scott* *June.*
marched with 500 *Light Infantry* and *Rangers*, taking a fatiguing Sweep through the Woods, to go to take Poſſeſſion of the *Light-houſe* Battery; and about 5, was followed by Brigadier *Wolfe*, with 4 Companies of Grenadiers commanded by Lieutenant-Col. *Hale*, and 1200 Men detached from the Line. They found this Battery deſtroyed by the Enemy, and but 4 pieces of Cannon left, which they had ſpiked up. A proper Quantity of Artillery, Tools, &c. was ſent thither by Sea. The *Situation* of the Place was the moſt advantageous that could be obtained, for annoying the *Iſland Battery*, and the *Ships*, with our Shot and Shells. On the Sea-ſide there was a little *Cove*, very convenient for landing Artillery and Stores for the Batteries to be erected here—beſides two ſmall *Encampments* deſerted by the Enemy, with their Tents ſtanding, in which were ſome Proviſions, Utenſils; and a great Quantity of cured Fiſh at *Lorembec*. All the landing Places here were defended with ſtrong *Breaſt-works* of the ſame Conſtruction with thoſe round *Kennington Cove*. At the *Cove*, where our Cannon was landed, there were two pieces of the Enemy's Cannon left with their Trunnions knocked

off, and at their *upper* Encampment 3 eight pounders, two of them ſpiked up. After Brigadier *Wolfe* had reconnoitred this Poſt, his whole Detachment incamped themſelves here about 4 in the Afternoon, and the *Light Infantry* and *Rangers* marched back to the *Grand Camp*.

June. 13. At Day-break this Detachment began to make a Road for carrying the *Artillery*, from the landing Cove, to the Spot fixed upon for a Battery. About 9 o'Clock this Camp was alarmed by a Meſſage from Major *Roſs*, who commanded a detached Guard at about a Mile and an half's diſtance, between the Camp and the Wood, that a large Party of the Enemy from the *Garriſon* was advancing towards his Poſt—upon which 4 Companies of Grenadiers, with a large Detachment from the *Line*, marched to ſuſtain the Major. But they ſoon ſaw, that the Enemy came only to burn ſome ſtraggling Houſes to the Eaſtward of the *Grand Battery* near the Beach of the Harbour, and then retreated peaceably into the *Garriſon*, as our Detachment did to the Camp at the *Light-houſe*.

The working Parties in the *Grand Camp* continued employed on the *Roads*, by Day, and during the Night in throwing up 3 *Redoubts*, on the Eminences from the Left to the Right. This Day a Body of about 300 Men made a *Sally* from the *Garriſon* upon their advanced Party—but in about an hour and an half they were repulſed by ſome few *Regulars* and**Light Infantry*.

The *Light-houſe* Camp being incommoded by the Enemy's Cannon from the *Iſland* Battery, about 9 o'Clock this Evening the *Line* removed to a Situation of greater Security—but the Grenadiers did not until Day-break.

This

This Day, and ſome others, the Service of landing the *Stores* and *Artillery* was interrupted by the exceſſive *Surf* upon the Shore, and many Boats were ſwamped, and ſome Proviſions damaged and loſt.

14. About Day-break, while the Grenadiers of the *Light-houſe* Camp were on their march in removing their Camp, they received Orders to ſuſtain Major *Roſs*'s Poſt, who had notice from the *Rangers*, that a Body of the Enemy appeared to move that way. But, before they joined him, Counter-Orders were iſſued to them, on ſeeing the Enemy retreating, having, as it appeared, intended nothing more than to alarm them. *June.*

This Day the Beſieged towed a *Sloop*, with two 24 pounders mounted on her Bows, into the Mouth of the Harbour, the better to annoy Brigadier *Wolfe*'s little Encampment near the Shore for landing his Artillery. She lay at Anchor near the *Iſland* Battery, fired her Cannon for ſome Hours, and then returned into the Harbour. She came to her Station again in the *Afternoon*, and fired for about an Hour and an half, with as little Damage to the Encampment, as before. She fired alſo upon the *Diana* Frigate and *Hunter* Sloop, that were ſtationed at Anchor as near the Harbour's Mouth as they could go with Security, to give the Alarm to Sir *Charles Hardy*'s Squadron, that lay farther out in the Offing, whenever the *French* Squadron ſhould make any Attempts to puſh out to Sea. The *Diana* returned the *Sloop's* Fire, but found the Sloop out of the Reach of her Metal; while the Sloop's heavier Metal reached her, and at times killed and wounded 6 of her Men. The *Diana* dared not to go nearer in, as the Sloop was covered by 10 two and forty pounders on the *Iſland*, pointed towards the Offing.

This

This Night ſeveral Pieces of *Cannon*, and ſome *Mortars* were landed for Brigadier *Wolſe*'s Detachment.

The working Parties at the *Grand Camp* were conſtantly employed upon the *Roads* and *Redoubts*, and in landing Artillery and Stores.—Thoſe three *Redoubts* were neceſſary to ſecure a Communication from the Right to the Left, in the Front of the Camp.

June. 15. There was a large Party at Work in drawing *Artillery* and carrying *Faſcines* and *Picquets* for the *Light-houſe* Battery. This Day 4 Mortars were ſhipped for the *Light-houſe*, with a Quantity of Proviſions and Stores from the Tranſports.

16. The working Parties were employed as the Day before——and upon the *Roads.*—No Artillery could yet be landed for the *Grand Camp.*

17. They were employed in the ſame manner. This Day two 8 Inch Mortars and 3 Royals, were ſent to the *Light-houſe* Camp.

18. This Morning the landing of Stores was interrupted by the great *Surf* driving on the Shore. In the Afternoon ſome 24 pounders were got on Shore. The working Parties of the *Grand Camp* were employed as before on the *Roads* for the Artillery.—The working Parties at the *Light-houſe* were employed in landing and drawing *Artillery*, and at Night in erecting *Batteries*, and mounting Cannon and Mortars.

This Night *L'Echo* Frigate of 32 Guns bound to *Quebec* with Stores and Proviſions got out of the Harbour, by the favour of a dark foggy Night, and a briſk Gale, which drove Sir *Charles Hardy* and his Squadron to Sea—Some of his *Frigates* chaſed, took and brought her in with them a Day or two afterwards.

19. Sir

19. Sir *Charles*'s Squadron returned to their Station off the Harbour's Mouth. The working Parties of the *Grand Camp* continued on the *Roads*, and in landing *Artillery* and *Stores*. *June.*

Between 9 and 10 this Night two Batteries, one of *Cannon* and one of *Mortars*, were opened at the *Light-house* upon the Ships in the Harbour, and upon the *Island* Battery, which continued a brisk Fire until Day-light, that was as briskly returned, but without any Damage on the *Light-house* side, on Account of the Height of its Situation, and the Shelter of Rocks and Hillocks. The *Bomb* Battery there consisted of 2 Mortars of 13 Inches Diameter, two of 8, and 6 Royals. At some Distance were 2 Hawitzers of 8 Inches, and small Batteries of one, two, and three Pieces of *Cannon*, 12 and 24 pounders, in all seven, properly disposed along the Shore to fire both *riochet* and *point-blank*. The whole Line marched to sustain the Batteries, if the Ship's Crews had made any Attempts to attack them. Part of the left Wing of the *Grand Army* and the *Light Infantry* were in Motion, to prevent any Parties out of the Garrison from attacking Brigadier *Wolfe*'s Detachment in flank. General *Amherst*'s Camp fired several times in the Night at the *Covert-way*, to divert the Attention of the Garrison to that side.

20. So warm a Fire from the *Light-house* was continued upon the Ships, that they judged it adviseable in the Afternoon to *warp in* about 600 Yards nearer to the Town; which was too great a Distance from our Batteries, to give them much Disturbance. At Night the *Mortars* there, were chiefly directed to the *Island* Battery. The Enemy burned an *old Ship* in the Harbour.

21. A

June. 21. A great Part of this Day there was a ſtrong Fire from the *Ships* towards the *Light-houſe* Battery, but without any Effect, but that of expending the Enemy's Ammunition—as there was alſo from the *Iſland* at Intervals, with as little Damage to our People or Batteries. The Ships fired ſeveral Shot into the left Wing of the *Grand Camp*, as did the *Garriſon* at the *Redoubts*, and the right Wing, and ſometimes at two or three People, and ſingle Paſſengers from one Place to another; but, without Effect.

The Mortars at the *Light-houſe* played briſkly on the *Iſland*; the Fire was returned from thence with 5 pieces of *Cannon* directed that way, and 2 ten Inch Mortars.

The working Parties were employed on the *Roads*, in landing *Stores* and *Artillery*, and in carrying Stores for the *Grand Camp*.

22. The *Grand Camp* improved the Advantage of this Day's *Fog*, as well as a Part of laſt Night in throwing up an advanced *Redoubt* between the Centre and Right *Redoubts*, to facilitate the Poſſeſſion of the *Green-hill*, the moſt commanding Eminence from the Camp-ſide of the Town, at the Diſtance of about 800 Yards from the *Glacis*, the eaſier to carry on their Approaches to the Walls.

Four hundred Men under the Command of Lieutenant Colonel *Hale* were employed to erect a Battery of ſix 24 pounders at the *Light-houſe*, to play upon the *Iſland*, whoſe Battery was frequently troubleſome, though it did no great Execution. This Day a *Block-houſe* was erected to ſecure the *Communication* to the *Light-houſe*.

The landing of Artillery and Stores was this Day interrupted by the exceſſive *Surf* on the Shore, and ſeveral Boats were ſwamped and ſtove.

23. A

23. A Company of Grenadiers worked hard on the new Battery at the *Light-houſe*——another Party was employed in erecting a Battery to play on the Ships from an Eminence behind the *Grand Battery*—the Ships gave frequent Interruptions to this Party. The Garriſon kept a pretty conſtant Fire directed towards the working Parties from the *Grand Camp*—as did the *Iſland-Battery* towards the *Light-houſe* Parties—the latter was chiefly returned in the Night time. *June.*

About this time they began the *Epaulement*, a Work for covering and facilitating the *Approaches* to the Town by the *Green-Hill*. This Work was about a *Quarter* of a *Mile* in length, about *nine* Feet high, and *ſixteen* Feet broad, made with *Gabions*, *Faſcines* and Earth, to be Proof againſt all Cannon Ball. It employed as many Men as could be ſpared for many Days; who, at the Beginning, were much interrupted by the Water of the very wet *Moraſs*, upon which they were obliged to make their *Road*, and to throw up this *Work*, with Earth brought from ſome diſtance.

Great Quantities of *Gabions* and *Faſcines* were landed and carried up for this *Work*, with all poſſible Speed and Diligence.

24. The working Parties were employed as the Day before, and with the ſame Interruptions. In the Park of Artillery, thirteen 24, and ſeven 12 pounders this Day.

25. The *Light-houſe* Battery opened at Day-light upon the *Iſland* with five 24 pounders: The Ships and the Iſland returned their Fire briſkly, and wounded one of their 24 pounders. In the Afternoon the Embrazures at the eaſt End of the *Iſland* Battery, appeared very much ſhattered by the Shot from the *Light-houſe*—Since 4 o'Clock this Afternoon,

noon, the Enemy fired only Shells from thence; which made our People ſuppoſe that moſt of the Guns that bore on the *Light-houſe*, were either wounded or diſmounted. The Battery at *Maurepas Point*, and the Men of War, kept a conſtant Fire directed that way; but with little or no Effect, on Account of the great Diſtance.

June. 26. The advanced Parties of the *Grand Camp* had a Skirmiſh with a reconnoitring Party of the Beſieged, who had come out to ſet Fire to the *Block-houſe*; but were ſoon forced back without effecting their Deſign. This Night our Troops got Poſſeſſion of the *Green-hill*, without any great Oppoſition, and with very little Loſs.

27. A more conſtant Fire of Guns and Mortars from the *Ships* and *Garriſon* upon our working and advanced Parties. The *Light-houſe* Battery now and then threw a Shell upon the *Iſland*, to prevent the Enemy from repairing their Works. A braſs 24 pounder was loſt in 12 Fathom Water, by ſliping off the *Float* for landing Artillery, they called *Catamaran*. This Day the *Admiral* ſent on Shore 200 *Marines*, or rather Troops ſerving as *Marines* on this Expedition, who took Poſt at *Kennington Cove*, and were a great Relief to the Army in Camp.

28. The Enemy kept a pretty conſtant Fire upon the *Grand Camp* and *Batteries*, with little Effect.

This Night they ſunk *two Frigates* and *two Store-ſhips* with a great Weight of Stones in them; they were faſtened together with Cables, and moored down with Anchors, in the narrow Entrance of their Harbour, to prevent more than one of our Ships at a time from getting in there, if we ſhould think it neceſſary at any time of the *Siege* to *force* the Harbour with our Fleet.

29. Some

29. Some *Indians* ſhewed themſelves and killed one of our Men—the *Light Infantry* purſued, killed and ſcalped two, and brought in another of them.

This whole Night the work of the *Epaulement* was much interrupted, by the briſk Fire the Enemy conſtantly made on our working Parties there. The greateſt Interruption they had was from *L'Arethuſe* Frigate, ſtationed as high up the Harbour on that ſide as the Depth of Water would permit, with her Broad-ſide bearing upon the low Paſs, by which our Troops were obliged to advance, to make their Approaches; which the *Epaulement*, when it was completed enabled them to do, with more Eaſe, and an inconſiderable Loſs.

30. A very briſk Fire from the *Ships* and *Garriſon* was made upon our working Parties. Some Shells were thrown from the Battery at *Maurepas Point*, and from the *Iſland* upon the Parties at the *Light-houſe*—In the Night theſe Parties worked very briſkly in drawing Cannon from the *Light-houſe*, about the Diſtance of *two Miles*, over uneven Ground never ſmoothed into a Road, to their *new* Batteries near the *Grand Battery*, to play upon the *Frigate* and the reſt of the *Ships*, and to remove them once more, if poſſible; that the *Grand Camp* might carry on their Approaches with the greater Security and more Expedition. Some People of the Garriſon, to expreſs their Surpriſe at this and ſome other Inſtances of the Suddenneſs of Brigadier *Wolfe*'s Motions from one Place to another, and their Sentiments of the Effect of his Opetions, uſed to ſay——There is no Certainty where to find him——but, wherever he goes, he carries with him a *Mortar* in one Pocket, and a 24 *pounder* in the other. *June.*

E 2 *July* 1.

July. *July* 1. Upon Intelligence received, that the Enemy's *Picquets* on a wooding Party of about 400 had in the Morning crept out about a Mile beyond the *Barrafoy*; Brigadier *Wolfe* at the Head of 100 *Light Infantry*, fupported by near 300 *Regulars*, with Orders left for the *Picquets* of the *Line* to advance, if neceffary, in about a quarter of an Hour came up with the Enemy; who made a Stand for about half an hour or better. But, being repulfed in this Skirmifh, they began to retreat from Hill to Hill, but in good Order, and firing frequently. Our Party purfued them all the while, referving their Fire till they came very near; when they gave them fo warm a *Salute*, that they made a precipitate Retreat to their former Poft. This Affair lafted about two Hours and an half, with only 6 or 8 of our Men wounded. By this Succefs the Brigadier became Mafter of two very advantageous Eminences, that he never quitted. A *Redoubt* was thrown up with all Expedition, to maintain the fartheft Poft; and a little nearer advanced, a *Redan*, within 400 Yards of the Enemy's Picquets, amidft a brifk cannonading both from the Town and the Ships. From this Situation our Batteries, without being much expofed, could play on the Ships at a good Diftance, and by that Means greatly facilitate the *Approaches* from the *Grand Camp*.

In the Afternoon a Party near the Right, after a flight Skirmifh, repulfed another Party of the Enemy towards Cape *Noir*, who attempted to furprize and interrupt our working Parties. The *Garrifon* continued a pretty conftant cannonading.

Some *Deferters* came in from the *Garrifon*, who were all fent on board the Fleet, that they might not have even a Poffibility of acting as *Spies* under the Pretence of being *Deferters*.

This

This Night *two* other *Frigates* were ſunk at the *Entrance* of the Harbour, very near the others—Part of almoſt all their *Top-maſts* appeared above Water.

2. There were about 100 *Marines* ſent on Shore *July.* from the *Admiral*'s Ship properly officer'd, to join Brigadier *Wolfe's* Party near the *Grand-Battery*.

3. Our Troops were now very indefatigable in forming their *Lines*,

4. Notwithſtanding the warm *cannonading* from the Beſieged every Day, *Five* hundred Men were conſtantly employed in making *Faſcines* for the *Roads* and *Epaulement*.

5. The faithful Partizans of the *French*, their few native *Indians*, ſhewed themſelves very watchful about the Edges of the Woods, by taking off ſome of the Tranſports Men that were too curiouſly adventurous, contrary to Orders, and intirely ignorant how to deal with ſuch a wary lurking Enemy. Sometimes they nabbed or carried off an Out-Centinel, after creeping through Weeds and Shrubs, and ſculking there for ſeveral hours together, to watch an Opportunity either of ſhooting, or ruſhing in a Body upon him unperceived, when his Back was turned.

Laſt Night Brigadier *Wolfe* began to play a Battery of 7 Pieces of *Cannon*, 12 and 24 pounders, and two 13 Inch *Mortars* on the *Ships*, while the reſt of his Party were very active in getting more Guns mounted.

6. The Vigilance and Activity of General *Amherſt*, and of the Brigadiers *Whitmore* and *Laurence* in forwarding their *grand Deſign* from the Campſide, was not diſcouraged or leſſened by the briſk, almoſt conſtant cannonading of the Beſieged, both from their *Ships* and *Garriſon*; which only took off a Man

a Man or two now and then, and at other times wounded ſome few others. The working Parties from the *Grand Camp*, always under the Inſpection of one of the *General* Officers, were conſtantly employed in forwarding the *Approaches*; while the advanced and covering Parties always maintained the Advantages they had already gained, and often poſſeſſed themſelves of more advanced Situations, to enable them with Succeſs to employ the vaſt *Train* of Artillery and Quantity of Stores of all Kinds, the Officers and Men of the Fleet had now landed from the Tranſports, in all the Places that were moſt convenient to their Roads. The *Approaches* to the Town were greatly delayed by *unavoidable* Cauſes—almoſt a continual *Surf* on the Shore of landing; the numerous *Bogs* neceſſary to be drained before any Roads could be made over them for Carriages to paſs; and the making of ſuch a Cover as the *Epaulement* from the Fire of the Ships in the Harbour, to which the moſt convenient *Paſs* of Approach was expoſed. Our *Army* had a Demonſtration how *neceſſary* it is to have a Squadron of Ships in that Harbour in the Time of a Siege; and the *Garriſon*, of how *little* other Service an *inferior* Squadron to that of the Beſiegers is, but to prolong the Day of *Capitulation*. All the Troops were in good Health and high Spirits, and ſuffered conſiderably leſs than might have been expected from the conſtant Cannonading of the Beſieged.

July. 7. Parties of the Troops were employed this Day as others had been on the former Days. Their *Indifference* to what the unexperienced might call a *dreadful Fire* from the Beſieged at Intervals, was very remarkable. They regarded the Enemy's frequent *Shot* and *Shells*, juſt *as little* as they did the

random

random Fire of their *Musquetry*; the *Shells* in general rather *less* especially in the *Night*, when they could easily discern the Line of their *Direction* by the Blaze of their *Fus es*—and if they suspected that they were within the Distance of a *bursting Shell*, they instantly threw themselves flat on their Faces upon the Ground, and almost always with Security—their greatest Danger was from a *Shell* that did not burst for *some time* after it fell—

8. This Night the Enemy made a vigorous *Sally* from Cape *Noir* about 11 o'Clock upon our advanced and working Parties at the Lines, where Brigadier *Laurence* commanded. The Salliers with a Body of about 900 Men, by the *Darkness* of the Night and the *Silence* of their Motions, were fortunate enough to pass unobserved by some of our *advanced* Parties commanded by Lord *Dundonal*, and to surprize the *working* Parties in the Trenches; who with some Difficulty retreated, as they had not their Arms to defend themselves. Our *covering* Parties no sooner heard their Fire, than they advanced, and, after a very brisk Opposition, bravely repulsed the Salliers in a little time, with the Loss of two *Captains* and 17 of their Men, wounded several others, and made some Prisoners; among whom was a *wounded Officer*, who some time afterwards lost his *Life* by his Wounds in our Hospital, because he would not part with a *Leg* to save it. The Loss our Parties sustained in this Skirmish, was a *Captain* and 5 Men killed, 17 wounded, and 11 made Prisoners, besides the *wounded Lieutenant Tew*, and Captain *Bontein* an Engineer. The Garrison sent our a *Flag* of *Truce* for time to bury their Dead.— *July.*

It is remarkable that the *Officers* and the *Party* on this *Sally*, owed what Resolution they shewed to

the

the flashy, temporary Courage inspired by *Claret*, which they had very plentifully guzzled before their Attempt, as appeared from the Intoxication of our Prisoners. Some *Deserters* reported, that no Parties could be found in the *Garrison*, forward enough to go on this Service, without being first animated by a sufficient Quantity of *Wine*.

July. 9. By Order of the *Admiral*, Volunteers for the Company of *Miners* were enquired for on board all the *Men* of *War*——All the Men who professed themselves acquainted with the use of the Spade and Pickax, shewed great Readiness to go on this Service—most of the Men on board. *L'Arethuse* Frigate was obliged to *haul* in close to the Town.

This Day Brigadier *Laurence* was *slightly* wounded by a piece of a Shell that burst at some Distance from him.

10. The *Volunteers* for the Company of *Miners* were sent on Shore from all the Ships to the *Captain* of the Party, about 200 in Number, who were incamped by themselves.

As the *Besiegers* every Day and Night continued to advance with their Works, the *Garrison* kept a brisk, constant cannonading, and threw several Shells. It is remarkable, that they discharged great Quantities of old Iron of several Kinds, (such as *Shovels*, *Tongs*, and the like, besides a most destructive Sort of square Iron-bars of about 5 or 6 Inches long, and about an Inch and a half square, several of them cased in Plates of Tin,) which they call *Mitraille*, by way of Grape Shot—the Wounds they give are very difficult, if at all, to be cured, from their being made with such angular, ragged Weapons.

This Night our People observed a *great Fire* in the Woods in sight of *Louisbourg*, which they rightly

rightly conjectured to be a Signal to the Garriſon of Monſ. *Boiſhibere*'s Arrival, who, as we learned by the Report of Deſerters, was expected about this time with a Party of *Canadians* and *Indians*, ſome to reinforce the Garriſon, and the reſt to harraſs the Rear of our Camp, and to watch Opportunities of cutting off all ſmall Parties of our Men, who might be accidentally detached to any diſtant Poſts. This *Chief* is well known to the Colonies at and about *Annapolis Royal* in *Nova Scotia*, for his own faithleſs Inhumanity, and for the miſchievous Activity and treacherous Cruelty of his lurking Parties.

11. Some of his Party ſeized a *Soldier* who was driving a Waggon to the left Wing of the Camp; from whom they extorted all the Intelligence he was able to give, by the Menaces of a ſpeedy *Execution* if he did not, or reported any thing they ſhould diſcover to be falſe. *July.*

12. However, by what Means is not very certain, he contrived to make his *Eſcape*, and after being ſome time purſued undiſcovered, returned to the Camp, and reported that the Party ſaid they were about 50 near the Place he was brought to, and to the Number of 200 farther in the Wood— and that they had with them a great many Head of *Cattle*.—

13. Our working Parties continued very indefatigable upon the Trenches; as did

14. The Beſieged in doing all that a briſk Cannonading could do, to force them from the Attempt, or at leaſt to leſſon their Numbers, in order to delay their Succeſs. The Batteries of the Beſiegers were traced out laſt Night.

15. In the Night the miſchievous Frigate *L'Arethuſe* taking the advantage of a dark Night and a thick *Fog*, got out of the Harbour, but not un-

 perceived

perceived by the *Light-house* Party, who made Signals with Rockets to Sir *Charles Hardy*'s Squadron; ſeveral of whom chaſed her, but at a great Diſtance, till they loſt Sight of her in a Fog impenetrable to human Eyes, and extended on this Coaſt for many a Score Leagues. Two or three of the *Deſerters* from our Camp were ſent to *France* in this Frigate—another had his Head ſhot off while he was very active on Duty in the Town.

July. 16. About 7 o'Clock this Evening, Brigadier *Wolfe* made himſelf Maſter of a Poſt occupied by the Enemy's *Picquets* within about 400 Yards of the *Weſt Gate*, where about 100 of their *Volunteers* had ſecured themſelves behind ſome ſmall *Breaſt-works* of Sand-Bags—He advanced towards this Poſt with only 8 or 10 Men, leaving Orders for a ſuſtaining Party to follow him from the *Green-hill*. Upon his approaching the Enemy, they fired ſome few Muſkets at him; when he diſpatched an Officer to the adjacent *Redan*, with Orders for an Officer and 20 of the *Light Infantry* to croſs the *Barraſoy* Bridge immediately, ſupported by 20 Grenadiers. They advanced with all Expedition one after another, at about 2 Yards diſtance from each other, and on the Bridge received three Fires from the Enemy's Breaſt-works, without any Loſs. On the *Light Infantry*'s advancing farther without firing their Pieces, the Enemy's Party retired with much Precipitation towards the *Weſt-Gate*, firing ſome random Shot in their Flight, and were purſued, without the Loſs of a Man, in the midſt of a warm Fire of grape and round Shot both from the *Town* and Ships, and from the ſmall Arms of the Rampart and Covert-way. At this Poſt the Brigadier made a good Lodgment. The Fire from the Beſieged was continued briſkly during the whole Night

Night after, with ſeveral Shells thrown at Intervals into the *new* Poſt he had gained; which was reinforced with 5 Companies of Grenadiers and 100 Highlanders under the Command of Lieutenant-Col. *Hale*.

This Night the Left of the *Lines* of *Approach* was *opened* by the very ſame Grenadiers, and the Remainder of their Company, with the Loſs only of 4 or 5 Men, and 7 or 8 wounded.

The Honourable Capt. *Edgcumbe* with 6 or 7 Ships replaced Sir *Charles Hardy*'s Squadron on the Station off the Harbour's Mouth.

17. The Parallel was extended from the Right to the Left with little Loſs, in the Face of a very hot Fire from the Beſieged. *July.*

A Deſerter from *Boiſhibere*'s Party came in, and ſaid, they had hanged 3 or 4 *Seamen* whom they had taken on the 5th belonging to the Tranſports.

This Evening Sir *Charles Hardy*, with ſome of his Squadron, returned to his Station—the *Frigate* was lucky enough to make her Eſcape—

18. There was a conſtant briſk Fire of Muſketry from the *Covert-way*, made by the Beſieged all laſt Night and this whole Day, upon our Parties on the *Lines*, who ſuffered very little from it. The *Garriſon* directed ſeveral of their Shells both in the Day and Night towards our *Laboratories* and *Magazines* in the *Grand Camp*—The Direction was given by the Information of a *Deſerter* from us.

More of the Tranſports Men were taken off by the Vigilance of ſome lurking *Indians* near the Shore in *Gabreuſe* Bay—One Warning was not enough for them.—

19. The *Lines* from the right and left Wing were *joined* by the Beſiegers—and our Batteries from the Left were opened and began to play with

Succeſs upon the Baſtion *Dauphine* at the Weſt Gate, notwithſtanding the briſk and conſtant Cannonading from the *Garriſon*; from which our People ſuffered much leſs than might have been expected.

July. 20. The Operations of the former Day were ſucceſsfully continued—In the Evening a Body of about 400 *Seamen* were ſent on Shore, and erected by the next Morning a very ſtrong *Battery* of 5 pieces of Cannon to the Right, without the Loſs of a Man. The Seamen were under the Direction of an *Engineer*, and commanded by a *Captain* of one of our *Frigates*, who were all to take their Turns at this Duty, as the *ſenior Captains* had done at that of landing the Artillery and Stores, with the *Lieutenants* of the Fleet in Rotation upon both theſe Services.

21. The Operations of this Day were much the ſame with thoſe of the two former ones—About 2 in the Afternoon, by a Shell from the *Light-houſe* Battery, as the moſt credible Priſoners declare, *Le Celebre* of 64 Guns in the Harbour was ſet on Fire, and after her *Allowance* of Powder on board *for the Day* blew up part of her Deck with a very loud Exploſion, ſhe burned with great Violence. As this Ship was burning, the Fire communicated itſelf to *L'Entreprennant* of 74 Guns, and from her ſpread itſelf to *Le Capricieux* of 64 Guns—There was no Exploſion from the two *latter* Ships, as the Men had been very briſk in throwing their *Powder* over-board, before the Flames could ſpread themſelves ſo far.—This muſt not be underſtood of the *Quantity* of Powder theſe Ships arrived with, as *complete* for Service—*That* they had taken out at the Beginning of the *Siege*, and lodged on board a *Store ſhip* not far from the Town, as a Precaution againſt the more dreadful Conſequence of an accidental

dental *Shell* from any of our Batteries falling into their *Magazines:* And every Night they carried on board each of the Ships the *Quantity* they judged would be *sufficient* for the Service of the following *Day*—This is what was above called their *Allowance* of Powder *for the Day.* As soon as the Fire reached their *Guns* that were loaded, some with round, some with grape *Shot*, they discharged themselves indiscriminately on *Friend* and *Foe*, some towards the *Town* and the *Battery* of the Besiegers, and others on their own *Ships* and *Boats.* Their Men with much Difficulty escaped on Shore in their Boats, through a brisk *Fire* from our Batteries added to the *accidental* Discharges of their own Ships Guns. The three Ships made a prodigious Blaze for the whole Night, and after burning down to the Water's Edge, quite loosed from their Moorings, they were by the Tide driven on Shore upon the Mud at the *Barrasoy* End of the Harbour, with all their Iron and Guns tumbled one upon another in their Holds, which will be saved by our People.

Le Prudent of 74 Guns, and *Le Bienfaisant* of 64, seeing this *casual* Burning of the *greater* part of their Squadron, warped off as fast as possible towards the other End of the Harbour, to be out of the Reach of the Flames from the other Ships; Fortune reserving their *Fate* some *few* Days longer.

22. About Sun-rise the Besiegers opened two other Batteries on the Right with thirteen 24 pounders, and another of 7 *Mortars*, to throw Shells into the *Covert-way* and *Ramparts*, from whence the Besieged kept Night and Day a very hot Fire with their *Musketry*, and they were not less active with their *Cannon* and *Mortars.* Another Battery from the Left, which was not 500 Yards off, played briskly *July.*

July. briſkly, and with ſo very viſible an Effect on the
22 Fortifications, that the Beſiegers had the encouraging Satisfaction to ſee the *Revêtement*, with a great Quantity of Earth tumbling down after the firing of moſt of their Shot.

There were three other Batteries from the North-ſide of the *Barraſoy* Bridge, one of 4, one of 5, and a third of 7 Pieces of *Cannon*, beſides 2 large *Mortars*, kept conſtantly playing on the Weſt Gate and its Cavalier, where ſome Guns were diſmounted; and at Intervals they were directed to the two remaining Ships in the Harbour, with exceeding good Effect every Way—The Officers of the Beſieged have ſince more than once declared, that they never ſaw any Artillery *better ſerved* than at this Siege—That there was hardly one of our *Shot*, that did not perform ſome Execution, and many of them from their judicious Direction did them as much Damage as was poſſible for any ſingle Shot to do. A Battery was begun on the Left for 4 twenty-four pounders.

Every Night ſince the near Approach to the Walls, there was a Party of our *Light Infantry* kept without the *Lines* near the Bottom of the *Glacis*, to prevent our working Parties on the Trenches and Batteries from being ſurprized by any ſudden *Sally* of the Beſieged.

The Batteries on the Right of the Lines played upon the *Citadel Baſtion* with ſuch Effect, that a Breach was very ſoon expected there. Several of our *Mortars* were ſerved with very great Succeſs—The Town was ſet on Fire ſeveral times by Shells thrown from the Right—ſome of the very firſt lighted moſt of the *Citadel* Buildings and the *new Barracks* into a prodigious Blaze.—Our Men were not a little rejoiced when they ſaw the *Church-Stee-*

ple

ple and *Spire* knocked down, as they had heard, that the Besieged constantly kept an *Officer* up there, to observe the Motions and Advances of the Besiegers from time to time,

This Night the *Seamen* were employed in erecting more advantageous, more advanced *Batteries*; which they did with great Spirit, and equal Success.

23. A brisk Cannonading was continued from *July.* all our Trenches with good Execution upon several Parts of the Fortification, besides that of the Cohorns, and of the *French* Mortars for throwing of Stones—and our Shells set the Town on Fire in several Places.

24. The Cannonading from our Trenches was continued with great Spirit and little Loss—and our Shells set the Town on Fire in several Places.

Another *Battery* was opened this Day to the Right of our Lines, to flank the *Citadel Bastion*— We have since learned, that several of the *Guns* on the *Ramparts* were about this time wounded, and several dismounted—and that *three* of the *Mortars* in the Garrison were rendered useless by a *single Shot* from one of our Batteries.

This Day the Fire from the Besieged slackened considerably——while ours increased with our additional Works and visible Success.

Some Deserters that came in to our Trenches this Day reported, that the *Inhabitants* of the Town were so much harrassed and distressed by our Shot and Shells, that they on their Knees *intreated* the Governor to *capitulate*—but, to no manner of Purpose.—Whatever Stress might be rested on this Report, most of our Men improved it to their own Advantage, that of keeping up their brave Spirits, with the very probable Prospect of the speedy

ſpeedy Reduction of a Place, that had given them ſo much Fatigue, and promiſed them ſo much Reputation. This Day the Fire of our *ſmall Arms* into the Embrazures of the *Ramparts*, drove the Enemy from their Guns.

July. 25. The Beſiegers were *indefatigable* in exerting their *Efforts* from the Trenches againſt the Fortifications, which had an exceeding good Effect. The *Citadel Baſtion*, and many of their *Embrazures* were very conſiderably damaged—and a large *Breach* was made in the Baſtion *Dauphine* at the *Weſt Gate*—which had encouraged them to bring their *Scaling Ladders* into the Trenches, that they might be ready for the very firſt favourable Opportunity of an *Eſcalade*, if that Extremity ſhould not be prevented by the ſpeedy *Surrender* of the Garriſon upon the formal *Summons* of the General.

About Noon, by the Admiral's Order, two *Boats*, a Barge and Pinnace or Cutter from every Ship, of the Fleet, except the *Northumberland*, an Invalid, manned only with their proper Crews, and armed with Muſquets and Bayonets, Cutlaſſes, Piſtols, and Pole-Axes, each Boat under the Direction of a *Lieutenant* and *Mate* or *Midſhipman*, rendezvouſed at the *Admiral*'s Ship: From thence they were detached by two's and three's at a time to join thoſe of Sir *Charles Hardy*'s Squadron off the Mouth of the Harbour. There they were in the Evening ranged in *two Diviſions* under the Command of the *two Senior Maſters* and *Commanders* in the Fleet, the Captains *Laforey* and *Balfour*.

In this Order they put off from Sir *Charles*'s Squadron about 12 o'Clock, and by the Advantage of the foggy *Darkneſs* of the Night, and the inviolable *Silence* of their People, paddled into the Harbour of *Louisbourg*, unperceived either by the

the *Island* Battery they were obliged to come very near to, or by the *two Men* of *War* that rode at Anchor at no great Diſtance from them. There was no great Probability of their being perceived from any Part of the *Garriſon*, not only on Account of their greater Diſtance, but alſo of the *preconcerted* briſk *Diverſion* made upon them from all our Batteries about that time. Beſides, the Beſieged themſelves left no body an Opportunity to hear any Noiſe: For, from having in the Day time obſerved the numerous *Scaling-ladders* that were brought into our Trenches, they were under ſome Apprehenſions of an *Eſcalade* intended as this Night, and kept a conſtant Fire with their Muſketry from the Ramparts during the whole time; with the Deſign, if poſſible, to deter the Beſiegers from that Attempt, by ſhewing them how well they were upon their Guard in all the Places it could probably be made. *July* 25.

During this ſeeming Security and prudent Precaution on both Sides, the bold Stratagem of the *Boats* for ſurprizing the *two remaining Ships* in the Enemy's Harbour, every Moment ripened for the Execution. After puſhing in as far almoſt as the *Grand Battery* leſt the Ships ſhould be too ſoon alarmed by their Oars, they took a Sweep from thence towards the Part of the Harbour, where the *Gentlemen* knew the Ships were, who had before very well reconnoitred it—and preſently diſcovered them. Each Diviſion of the *Boats* was no ſooner within Sight and Hail of the noble Object of their Attempt, Capt. *Laforey*'s of *Le Prudent*, and Capt. *Balfour*'s of *Le Bienfaiſant*, than, while the Centinels on board having hailed

July them in vain, began to fire on them, each of
25 the *Commanders* ordered his Boats to *give way along-ſide* their reſpective *Ships*, and to board them immediately with all the Expedition and good Order they could obſerve.

The *Boats Crews* no longer able to contain themſelves in Silence, after their Manner, gave *loud Cheers* as they were *pulling up along-ſide*, and with the moſt intrepid Activity, armed ſome with Muſkets, Bayonets and Cutlaſſes, others with Piſtols, Cutlaſſes and Pole-axes, followed their brave *Leaders* and boarded the Ships in an Inſtant with great Spirit, on each Bow, Quarter and Gang-way—and after very little Reſiſtance from the terrified Crews, ſoon found themſelves in Poſſeſſion of *two fine Ships* of the Enemy, one of 74, and one of 64 Guns, with the Loſs of very few of the *Seamen*, and but one *Mate*.

The Beſieged were now ſufficiently alarmed on all Sides by the *Noiſe* of the *Seamen* at boarding, the *Cheers* leaving them no Room to doubt that it was from *Engliſh Seamen*, and the Direction of the confuſed Sound of *Voices* and *Firing* afterwards ſoon leading them to ſuſpect the real Fact, an Attempt upon their Ships. The heroic, ſucceſsful Adventurers were employed in ſecuring their *Priſoners* in the Ships Holds, and concerting the moſt effectual Methods for ſecuring their *Prizes* out of the Reach of the enraged Enemy; when both the *Ships* and *Boats* received a moſt furious Fire of Cannon, Mortars and Muſkets from all Parts that it could be directed to them, from the *Iſland Battery* at no great Diſtance, from the Battery on *Point Maurepas* a little farther off and from all the Guns of the *Garriſon*

that

that could be brought to bear on that Part of the Harbour. *July.* *25*

After endeavouring in vain to tow off *Le Prudent*, they found ſhe was on ground, with ſeveral Feet Water in her Hold. There now remained nothing in their Power to do, to prevent her being recovered by the Enemy, but to ſet her on Fire—which they did with all poſſible Expedition, leaving along ſide her a *large Schooner*, and her *own Boats*, for her People to eſcape in to the Shore, which was at no great Diſtance from her. On board of this Ship they found a *Deſerter* from our Camp, who was killed in the little Buſtle at our People's taking Poſſeſſion of her, and by that Means reſcued from the ignominious Execution of *military Juſtice.*

The Boats from *Le Prudent* now joined the others about *Le Bienfaiſant*, and helped to tow her off triumphantly in the midſt of a formidable Fire from the mortified Enemy; which they did with great Speed by the Aſſiſtance of a little Breeze, and what ragged Sails, Yards and Rigging ſhe had left of any Service after the conſtant Fire ſhe had ſo long received from our Batteries. When they had thus got her out of the Diſtance and Direction of the Enemy's Guns, they *ſecured* her till the next Day by an Hawſer in the N. E. Harbour, and enjoyed on board her the firſt joyful Moment's Leiſure of ſecurely *congratulating* each other on their Succeſs and Safety in this hazardous Enterprize.

The taking of theſe two *Ships* by our Fleet's *Boats* on this *memorable* Occaſion, as it muſt be a laſting, indelible *Honour* to the Vigilance and Activity of thoſe who projected, and to the

July. *Bravery* and *Conduct* of those who executed, the
25 *bold* Design, will also be a *new*, and perhaps a *seasonable* Conviction to the whole World, that, however *arduous*, however *apparently-impracticable* any proposed *naval* Attempt may be, the *English Seamen* are not to be deterred from it by any Prospect of Difficulty or Danger, but will exert themselves as far as *Men* can do, and at least *deserve* Success, when led on to it by such as are *worthy* to command them.

Whether it may be *useful*, is not so certain as, that it is *just*; to observe in this Place, that at the Time of this *naval Assault*, there was neither *Captain* or *Lieutenant* on board either of these Ships, but an *Ensign* only in each left with the Command:——That their Decks were strewed about a Foot high with *Tobacco Leaves*, and large Pieces of *Junk*, as a Precaution to lessen the violent Effects of our *smaller Shells* that might accidentally alight in them:——And, that all their Sides within, were nailed over with *thick Nettings*, to prevent some of the Mischiefs from Splinters occasioned by Shot through their Sides. They had much greater Experience of the real Use of the *latter* Expedient, than of the *former*, during the Course of this Siege: For, you have seldom seen Ships more shattered with Shot-holes, especially on one side, with their Masts *standing*, than these two were, at the time they fell into our Possession:——*Shells* indeed none of the Ships received many of; and what happened to hit them, were none of the *largest* Sort, and but by Accident could have done them the Mischiefs they suffered.

26. Capt.

26. Capt. *Laforey*'s intrepid Conduct in the heroic Action of last Night was very justly rewarded with *Post* in *L'Echo* Frigate of 32 Guns, taken from the Enemy on the 19th of *June* last, as he was unfortunately obliged to set his own fine Capture *Le Prudent* on Fire, otherwise it is not doubted, that he would have been distinguished with the Command of that Ship——as Capt. *Balfour*'s was with that of *Le Bienfaisant*, which was immediately repaired with all Diligence, to be sent to *England*. *July.*

About low Water this Day *Le Bienfaisant* was on ground, at the Place where she was secured in the dark of the Morning, upon a soft Mud: And, soon after she began to *heel*, her Main, Mizen and Fore-topmasts had been so much wounded by the Shot from our Batteries, that they *went over* her Side, leaving her the horrid Appearance of a wrecked, as well as a conquered, Ship. Indeed, when our Ships came into the Harbour, there was hardly any Part of it, which had not the Appearance of Distress and Desolation, and presented to our View frequent Pieces of Wrecks and Remnants of Destruction—Five or six Ships *sunk* in one place with their Mast-Heads peeping out of the Water—the *stranded* Hull of *Le Prudent* on the muddy Shoal of the other side, burned down to the Water's Edge, with a great deal of her Iron and Guns staring us in the Face—Buoys of slipped Anchors *bobbing* very thick upon the Surface of the Water in the Channel towards the Town——a Number of small Craft and Boats towards that Shore, some intirely *under* Water, others with part of their Masts standing *out of* it; besides the *stranded* Hulls, Irons and Guns of

July. of the *three Ships* burned on the 21ſt, upon the
26 Mud towards the *Barraſoy*——and in the N. E. Harbour little elſe to be ſeen but Maſts, Yards and Rigging *floating up and down*, and Pieces of burned Maſts, Bowſprits &c. driven to the Waters Edge, and ſome Parts of the Shore edged with the *Tobacco Leaves* out of ſome of the Ships that had been deſtroyed——the whole a diſmal Scene of total Deſtruction!

This Day as the Fire of the *Beſiegers* was rather *briſker* than uſual, that from the *Garriſon* was but very *faint*——and that *diſcontinued* about 10 o'Clock in the Morning; when an *Officer* with a *Flag* of *Truce* was ſent out to General *Amherſt*, to deſire Terms of *Capitulation.*

It was Mr. *Boſcawen*'s conſtant Method from the very firſt Forenoon of landing the Troops in the Iſland of *Cape-Breton*, to go on Shore himſelf ſome part of the Day, and ſometimes twice every Day, if the *Buſineſs* of the Fleet, and the violent *Surf* on the Shore would permit him, into the *Grand Camp:* And, as on theſe Accounts his going *himſelf* was ſometimes uncertain, he had at leaſt one of his *Officers* every Day on Shore continually attending on General *Amherſt*, ſometimes to carry *Diſpatches* to him, and always to bring *Intelligence* from him of the whole Proceedings and Operations of the *Siege.*

The *Admiral* was this Day arrived at the *Head-Quarters*, but a few Minutes before the *Officer* came from the Garriſon to the *General*, and concerted with him the Nature of the *formal Summons*, to be ſent into the *Governor* of *Louisbourg*, to *ſurrender* the *Garriſon*. The *Admiral* had brought along with him ſomewhat of this Kind ready

ready drawn up in *English* in the Form of a *Letter*; the Contents of which were communicated to the *French Officer*. The *only Term* of *Capitulation*, which was delivered to him, was conceived in very few Words, to this Effect, that the Garrison must expect *no other Terms*, but to *surrender at Discretion*. There were *two Hours* time allowed the Governor for Deliberation.— *July.* 26

About the Expiration of the Time limited, there came *another Officer* from the *Governor*, with Remonstrances against the Hardship and Severity of *this*, importuning some other *more favourable Conditions.* After some little Consultation between the *Admiral* and *General*, they concluded upon this Condescension, that the Expression *at Discretion*, should be softened into, *Prisoners of War*—And, their generous Humanity added, 'That the Women and Children, and such of the Inhabitants of *Louisbourg*, as had not borne Arms, should be sent into *France*, in the Ships of his *Britannic Majesty*.' The *Officer* was assured, that *no other* Conditions whatever would be granted to the Garrison, who should be indulged an *Hour* longer for deliberating on these, but must expect no more Time to be given them.

Before the Expiration of this, a *Lieutenant-Colonel* was sent out to the *General Officer* in our Trenches, to propose that the *Officers* of the Garrison, upon *surrendering* themselves *Prisoners* of *War*, might be permitted to go to *France* instead of *England* upon their *Parole* given of *not serving* for a Time to be specified by the *General*.—On finding this could not be obtained, he desired the Favour of *one Hour* more for farther

July. 26 ther Deliberation.——The Answer he received from Brigadier Gen. *Whitmore*, was to this Purpose, 'That He was not at Liberty to suffer any more Messages to be carried to the *General* and *Commander in Chief*——but, that he would take it upon himself, to allow the Garrison one *quarter of an Hour* more, which they must *not exceed* on any Pretence; as he would certainly begin to renew his Fire upon them, if he heard no more from the *Governor*, when that Time was expired.' When it was very near up, a *Lieutenant-Colonel* came running out of the *Garrison*, making Signs at a Distance, and bawling out as loud as he could, *We accept*—*We accept*——He was followed by two *others*; and they were all conducted to General *Amherst*'s Head-Quarters.

The Besiegers had this Morning completed some other strong Batteries, which the *Surrender* of the *Garrison* had timely prevented them from *opening*. There was already a very considerable Breach made in the Wall at the *West Gate*; and the Works were so very much battered and damaged in several other Parts, that the Besiegers had meditated a *Storm* and *Escalade* as this Night, or the following at farthest—The *Fleet* was to have attacked the Garrison from the side of the *Harbour*; while the *Army* assaulted it from the *Camp* side. The Besieged had already experienced the inflexible Bravery of *both* in *two* very astonishing, successful Enterprizes; and no one can wonder, if they were now too much terrified to hazard the Success of a *third* to their *united*, exasperated Efforts; the dreadful Consequence of which with too much Probability to be apprehended, would be the Extirpation of the whole

Garrison,

Garrison, and all the *Inhabitants* of the Town—Wisely to prevent this, they surrendered on the following *July.* 20

Articles of Capitulation

Between their Excellencies Admiral Boscawen *and Major General* Amherst, *and his Excellency the Chevalier de* Drucour *Governor of the Island of* Cape Breton, *of* Louisbourg *and of the Island of* St. John, *and their Appurtenances.*

I. THAT the Garrison of *Louisbourg* shall be *Prisoners of War*, and shall be carried to *England* in the Ships of his *Britannic* Majesty.

II. All the Artillery, Ammunition, Provisions, as well as the Arms of every Kind whatsoever, which are at present in the Town of *Louisbourg*, the Islands of *Cape Breton*, and *St. John's*, and their Appurtenances, shall be delivered, without the least Damage, to such Commissaries as shall be appointed to receive them, for the Use of his *Britannic* Majesty.

III. The Governor shall give his Orders, that the Troops which are in the Island of *St. John* and its Appurtenances, shall go on board such Ship of War as the *Admiral* shall send to receive them.

IV. The Gate called *Porte Dauphine* shall be given up to the Troops of his *Britannic* Majesty to-morrow at eight o'Clock in the Morning, and the Garrison, including all those that carried Arms, drawn up at Noon on the *Esplanade*, where they shall lay down their Arms, Colours, Implements and Ornaments of War. And, the Garrison ſhall go on board, in order to be carried to *England* in a convenient Time.

V. The ſame Care ſhall be taken of the Sick and Wounded that are in the *Hoſpitals*, as of thoſe belonging to his *Britannic* Majeſty.

VI. The Merchants and their Clerks that have not carried Arms, ſhall be ſent to *France*, in ſuch Manner as the *Admiral* ſhall think proper.

(Signed)

Camp before *Louiſbourg*. *Edward Boſcawen.*
26th *July* 1758. *Jeffery Amherſt.*

The Counter part of theſe *Articles* was tranſlated into the *French* Language on the Part of the Governor, and

Dated at *Louiſbourg* (Signed)
the 26th of *July*, 1758. Le Chevalier de *Drucour.*

After the *Capitulation* was ſigned, the *General* detained a *Lieutenant-Colonel* of the Garriſon as an Hoſtage for the Articles being fulfilled on the Part of the Governor, until 8 o'Clock in the Morning of the

July. 27. When Major *Farquhar* with three Companies of Grenadiers took Poſſeſſion of *Porte Dauphine.* And, at Noon Brigadier-General *Whitmore* received in Form the Surrender of the Garriſon on the *Eſplanade*, directed their *Arms* and *Colours* to be carried out of the Town, poſted the neceſſary Guards and Centinels over the Stores, Magazines, &c. in the Town, and afterwards continued in the Garriſon, and acted as Governor of *Louiſbourg.*

It would be a great Omiſſion not to acquaint you, that all the *Officers* and *Men* on this *Expedition*, received from their *General* a public Teſtimony of his Approbation of their *gallant Behaviour*, which he he aſſured them ſhould be faithfully reported to their Royal Maſter.

It may be ſatisfactory to you, to receive the RETURN of the *Killed* and *Wounded* at the landing of the Troops on 8th *June*.

Of the ARMY.

Killed	Captain	Subalterns	Serjeants	Corporal	Private	Wounded	Subalterns	Serjeants	Corporal	Private	Miſſing
Total	1	3	[illegible]	1	41	Total	5	2	1	52	1

Of the NAVY.

Killed	Seamen	Died of wounds	Wounded	Lieutenants.	Mates or Midſh.	Seamen
Total			Total			

Of the TRANSPORTS.

Killed	Mates	Men	Wounded	Mates	Men
Total			Total		

N. B. Boats of the Men of War and Tranſports ſwamped and ſtove, about 130.

What *Forms* you ſee *not filled up*, are left for you to ſupply, when there is fuller *Intelligence*. Thoſe you ſee already *filled up*, you may depend on, as far as can be done on the Accuracy of *Tranſcribers*.

A Return *of the* Killed *and* Wounded *of the* Fleet, *on the 25th of* July, *in taking the Ships in the Harbour.*

Killed	Mates or Midſh.	Men	Wounded	Mates or Midſh.	Men
Total	1	6	Total	—	9

A Return *of the* Killed *and* Wounded *of the Troops between the Day of Landing, and the Surrender of* Louiſbourg.

The Killed	Commiſ. Officers. Captains	Commiſ. Officers. Lieutents.	Commiſ. Officers. Enſigns	Non-co. Officers Serjeants	Non-co. Officers Corporals	Non-co. Officers Drums	Private	The wounded.	Commiſ. Officers Captains	Commiſ. Officers Lieutents.	Commiſ. Officers Enſigns	Non-co. Officers Serjeants	Non-co. Officers Corporals	Non-co. Officers Drums	Private
Total	2	8	2	3	7	—	146	Total	4	16	3	4	3	2	315

Of the Artillery.

Killed	Gunner	Matroſſes	Wounded	Corporal	Gunn.	Matroſ.
Total	1	3	Total	1	1	5

This Return was tranſcribed by myſelf from an authentic Copy at large, as was alſo

The

The State *of the* Garrison *of* Louisbourg *on the Day it was surrendered.*

Names of the *Regiments*, and Numbers of the *Garrison*.	Officers.	Soldiers fit for Duty.	Sick and wounded.	Total of each Regiment.
24 Companies of *Marines* of the usual Garrison, and 2 Companies of the *Artillery* —	76	746	195	1017
Second Battal. of *Volontaires Etrangers*	38	402	86	526
D° *Cambise*	38	460	104	608
D° *Artois*	32	407	27	466
D° *Bourgogne*	30	353	31	414
Total of the Garrison	214	2374	443	3031
Sea Officers and Seamen	135	1124	1347	2606
Total Prisoners of War	349	3498	1790	5637

Authentic Accounts make the Number of their Killed, 2400 at the least.

The Artillery, Ammunition *and warlike Stores found in the* Garrison *and its* Batteries.

Muskets with Accoutrements	7600
Barrels of Powder	600
Musket Cartridges	8000
Musket Balls in Tons	13
CANNON.	**N°.**
French 36 Pounders, Iron	38
24 - - - -	97
18 - - - -	33
12 - - - -	19
8 - - - -	10
6 - - - -	28
4 - - - -	6
Total N°.	231
SHOT.	
For 36 Pounders	1607
24 - - - -	1658
12 - - - -	4000
6 - - - -	2336
GRAPE-SHOT.	
For 36 Pounders	139
24 - - - -	134
12 - - - -	330
6 - - - -	136

Case-Shot.	N°.
For 24 pounders - -	53
Double-headed Shot	
For 24 Pounders -	345
12 - - - -	153
MORTARS with Beds. Brass Inches 12½ Diam^r.	3
9 - - - -	1
6½ - - - -	3
	Iron
Inches 12½ Diameter	6
11 - - - -	4
9 - - - -	1
Total N°.	18
SHELLS.	
Inches 13 Diameter	805
10 - - - -	38
8 - - - -	158
6 - - - -	27
Total N°.	1028
COLOURS - - - -	11

An Account of the Ships *in the Harbour of* Louisbourg, *when the Troops landed.*

Names	Guns	What became of them.
Le Prudent	74	Taken by Boats 25th *July*, and afterwards burned.
L'Entreprennant	74	Burned by a Shell 21st *July*.
Le Celebre	64	The same Fate
Le Capricieux	64	The same Fate.
Le Bienfaisant	64	Taken by Boats 25th *July*, and commissioned.
L' Apollon	44	Sunk in the Harbour.
L' Echo	32	Taken by Sir *Charles Hardy*'s Squadron 18th *June*, and commissioned.
*L' Arethuse	36	Made her Escape in a Fog 15th *July*.
La Fidelle	26	Sunk in the Harbour.
Le Chevre	22	Sunk in the Harbour.
Le Biche	16	Sunk in the Harbour.
N. B. Besides La Dian	32	Taken by Sir *Charles Hardy*'s Squadron 25th *April*, and sold for the Benefit of the Captors.

As you expect me to give you some Account of the *Place*, as well as of the *Siege*; the following is the best in my Power to send you in this Hurry.

The Town of Louisbourg

LIES on the S. W. side of its Harbour, and consists of several narrow, paltry, stinking *Lanes* they call *Streets*. There is hardly a tolerable *House* in it, besides those of the *Governor* and *Intendant*, that are built of Stone and Brick without any Elegance. The best of all its Buildings are, the *Hospital*, *Nunnery*, and the *Magazines*.—Its fine *Barracks* built by the *English* during the last War, were all burned down by the *Shells* thrown into them during the Siege. Few of the other Houses, which were much damaged by the *Shot* of the Besiegers, are more than a better Sort of *boarded Cottages* a Story high; in which one could not help observing many Marks of the *shewy*

Beggary

Beggary of their late Inhabitants——to ſay nothing of the *Dirt* and *Slovenlineſs* of that *naſty fine* People whom the *Engliſh* ape with ſo much Fondneſs, and ſo little Taſte.

The Fortifications

Are as *regular* as the Situation would admit. Beſides a good *Rampart*, with irregular *Baſtions* and a *Cavalier* on one of them, it has a good *dry Ditch*, except towards the *Baſtion Dauphine*, where there is Water. The *Revêtement* of the Walls is not capable of ſtanding any long Battering, for Want of a *good Cement*; which is not to be made with *Sea-ſand*, and a *ſcanty* Allowance of *Lime*. The *Covert-way* and its *Traverſes* are pretty good, and the *Glacis* excellent. Before two of the *Curtains* there is a *Ravelin* with a *Bridge* to the *Sally-ports*. But, after all, the *Thickneſs* of its Walls, and the impaſſable *Moraſſes* from the Foot of its Glacis to a conſiderable diſtance, are what conſtitute the *Strength* of the Place more than the *Regularity* of its Works, or all the Pieces of *Cannon* that can be mounted on its Ramparts.

The Siege

Of this Place had nothing more *remarkable* in it, than the following Circumſtances——The *Engliſh* Forces landed in a Place, where it was but barely *poſſible*, tho' hardly *credible* without ſuch a ſucceſsful Conviction, for an Handful of Men, at the Time *defenceleſs* and *expoſed*, to ſucceed in the Face of Numbers, ſo advantageouſly *ſituated*, and ſo impregnably *fortified*.——The ſtrict Union, conſtant Harmony, and mutual good Inclination that ſubſiſted between the *Fleet* and *Army* in this *Expedition*, were inforced both by the Orders and *Examples* of the *Commanders* in *Chief*, and punctually obſerved by all their ſubordinate Officers. As this good Underſtanding contributed ſo much to their mutual

mutual *Happineſs*, as well as to the *Succeſs* of their united Efforts, in this joint Enterprize; it will always be remembered to their *Honour*, as almoſt the *only* Inſtance of ſuch *Unanimity* for a long Time between a *Fleet* and an *Army* ſent to act in Conjunction, upon Service of whatever Importance to the Public.——The well projected Deſign no leſs happily executed of ſurprizing and ſeizing in their very ſtrong Harbour *two capital Ships* of the *French*, by the Secrecy, Suddenneſs and Vigour of the *Coup de Main* of the *Boats* of the *Engliſh* Fleet; which will deſervedly make a memorable Article in the Annals of *Europe* for the Year 1758.——And, the very inconſiderable Number of Men the *Siege* of *Louiſbourg* coſt the *Engliſh*; which was much ſhort of what might reaſonably have been expected in the ſingle Attempt of *Landing*, where the *French* had ſuch fortified Lines, manned with ſuch powerful Numbers.

The Conqueſt of Louiſbourg

Is ſaid to be *peculiarly* remarkable for this *one* Obſervation—That the Humanity and Generoſity of our Commanders in *Chief* towards its *Garriſon* and *Inhabitants*, had more the Appearance of tranſplanting an *Engliſh Colony*, than the Behaviour of diſpoſſeſſing a *French Settlement*: And you would have believed the *Indulgences* granted to all of them, to have been ſhewn towards *Friends*, had you not been aſſured they were conferred upon *Priſoners*.

Wherever Succeſs and Victory may hereafter decide in Favour of any *French Commanders*; it is to be hoped, they will always remember the generous Treatment *all* their *People* received from the Conquerors of *Louiſbourg*.——It is not to be doubted, that the whole World will admire the ſuperior Greatneſs of the *Engliſh Commanders*, in ſo ſoon forgetting the barbarous Uſage of both their *Officers* and *Men* by the Ravagers of Fort *William-Henry*.

F I N I S.

www.ingramcontent.com/pod-product-compliance
Ingram Content Group UK Ltd.
Pitfield, Milton Keynes, MK11 3LW, UK
UKHW041952190726
13854UKWH00005B/1924

9 781845 743437